R O X

GW00670990

CURIOSITY KILLED THE CAT

The author would like to thank the
following for their help and assistance
in the production of this book:

Ian Westwater and the camera crew, Bill
Padgett and the lighting crew, and all the
other Geordie gentlemen on the floor of
The Roxy at Tyne Tees Television, for
allowing me to poke around with my
cameras and for being so helpful. Also
Betty, John and Thomas the Floor
Managers for being so tolerant. Alastair
Pirrie and the production staff of *The Roxy*
for sparing the time to talk to me,
especially in the early days of the show
when the heat was on. Diana, Alan, Mark
and Nick of Reflections Colour Lab, Lane
End, Bucks, for seeing my films through
on time and getting me out of some tight
spots with their skill. Jack Cutter, Norman
Stafford and John White, the
photographers at Tyne Tees, for all their
help and assistance and for allowing me to
use some of their pictures in this book.
Finally, Georgina Bangay, who gave up
part of her holiday from school teaching to
research the pictures and check the proofs.

First published in Great Britain in 1987
by Sidgwick & Jackson Limited
1 Tavistock Chambers, Bloomsbury Way
London WC1A 2SG

Copyright © 1987 by Joe Bangay
Introduction copyright © 1987 by
David Jensen

Designed and produced
by Grub Street Design, London
Art director: Roger Hammond
Designer: Graeme Andrew

All rights reserved. No part of this
publication may be reproduced, stored in a
retrieval system, or transmitted in any
form or by any means, electronic,
mechanical, photocopying, recording or
otherwise, without the prior written
permission of the copyright owner.

ISBN 0 283 99602 1

Typesetting by
Chapterhouse, The Cloisters, Formby,
Merseyside L37 3PX

Printed by Blantyre, Glasgow.

THE ROXY BOOK

JOE BANGAY

INTRODUCTION BY DAVID JENSEN

ECHO AND THE BUNNYMEN

SIDGWICK & JACKSON
LONDON

CONTENTS

DEF LEPPARD

THE CURE

LIVING IN A BOX

T SHOP BOYS

INTRODUCTION

MY SORT OF MUSIC SHOW

BY DAVID (KID) JENSEN

DAVID JENSEN AT *THE ROXY*

PRESENTING *The Roxy* on television is the sort of job I dreamed about when I was working as a sixteen-year-old radio jock on a little FM station in British Columbia. I was introducing a classical music programme on Saturday nights, and during breaks I would talk about English pop music to an English news copywriter who worked on the station and who used to play me his records. It was there that I really began to think about making a career in pop music and having my own programme, an idea reinforced when I met Radio Caroline DJ Steve Young when he visited Vancouver.

He had a scrapbook full of pictures of himself and various stars, and was full of stories about life as a DJ. He also played me the latest records from England and described *Top of the Pops*, then two years

old, which seemed a smart way to present pop music. About the same time I saw an episode of *Danger Man*, the hit TV series in which Patrick McGoohan was playing a pirate DJ. It was at about that moment in time that the plan for me to go to university and become an oceanographer went out of the window.

When I became a DJ in Europe and later on Radio One at the BBC in London, I worked on various TV music shows like *45* at Granada, *Pop Quest* for Yorkshire TV, and later on *Razzmatazz* for Tyne Tees Television. I also did *Top of the Pops* at the BBC and presented the first live show from Manchester.

When I was offered the Network Chart Show and my own morning show on Capital Radio in London, I decided to leave the BBC – it was time for a change and the attraction of the Chart Show was irresistible.

It may have been a coincidence, but shortly before I joined Capital I had a call from the *Tube*'s producer at Tyne Tees, asking if I was prepared to be their man to present a chart show on television. This was even before they knew they were doing it! For three years the chart show remained just a pipe dream. When I was working on *Razzmatazz* up in Newcastle, I was always talking about it to the producers and asking when would it happen. Tyne Tees were already into their five-year run of the *Tube* and their production teams and camera crews were heavily committed. When the *Tube* ended, Tyne Tees continued planning the chart show in the face of fierce competition.

I remember getting a phone call one Tuesday evening from Alastair Pirrie, producer-designate of the planned show. He sounded very low and miserable. 'I've got some news for you,' he said. I waited, not suspecting a wind-up, when suddenly his voice screamed down the phone 'We've got it!' The chart show was on.

With only three weeks to the first transmission on 9 June, there was so much to do. We still needed a second presenter to work with me. Kevin came up to Newcastle, charmed everybody, landed the job, and started working almost immediately. We did dummy production runs and, even up to the last few days, had many meetings to decide which bands would do the first show.

On the opening day we were faced with an air strike, which complicated travel arrangements, and problems with the new editing equipment that plays such a huge part in the show.

The criteria I have for any show I work on is that it must be the sort of show I would like to watch myself.

We try to get in seven musical items each week, with only a little chatting to link the items, with the objective of keeping it very well-paced. The content of the show, which I regard as an entertainment, will vary a little each week to cater for various tastes.

We try to please every sort of pop fan by having a wide range of acts, from Echo and the Bunnymen to artists like Kim Wilde and Shirley Bassey.

The Roxy is more successful than *Top of the Pops* because the bands forget that it is a studio and regard it as a live gig in a club. You can see from their faces how much they are enjoying it. To me there is a subtle, more personal difference. On *Top of the Pops* I was just the presenter but at *The Roxy* I am part of a small, tightknit production team that is like a family. We all air our views and criticisms are freely offered and discussed. We talk to each other constantly on the phone about the show. Each Friday Kevin and I have a meeting in London with some of the production team to decide on the acts to be invited for the following week.

Some of the acts I have watched on *The Roxy* have really impressed me. I thought Def Leppard were terrific. They entered into the spirit of the show and really got the crowd with them. Echo and the Bunnymen are committed fans of *The Roxy* and gave a great performance, while Terence Trent D'Arby was really powerful and had the girls in the audience hooked. New Order, who were the first band to play live, were tremendous and had a great concert hall sound. I just hope Elvis Costello, one of my favourites, gets a hit and comes on the show.

This book is a pictorial record of the first exciting months of our new show. It also tells you a little about the people who make the show and a great deal, which you may not know, about many of the artists and bands who have appeared on *The Roxy* stage. Joe Bangay, who is a Fleet Street music photo-journalist, covered the *Tube* for several years and took most of the pictures in the book. He has been keeping an eye and his camera pointed at *The Roxy* since it began, recording the antics of the artists on stage and off.

I hope you find our first Christmas *Roxy Book* interesting and will make a New Year's resolution to keep watching the show.

NEAR DISASTER FOR FIRST SHOW

*T*HE *Roxy* has very quickly become the shop window for all that is exciting in British rock and pop music since its first transmission in June this year. Twice a week it brings to the public the best of the current chart music, played by both established stars and rising new talents. With its audience climbing every week it is now established as the most successful chart show on the box. Yet it was touch and go as to whether the show would reach the TV screens on its scheduled opening night.

Tyne Tees Television were given only three weeks to get the show ready, after heavy lobbying and fierce independent competition had threatened to take from the creators of *Razzmatazz* and the *Tube* the show they had always been promised. To make matters worse, an unexpected strike by air traffic control assistants on launch day had grounded all internal flights in Britain. This left presenters and artists in various parts of Britain and Eire, struggling to find ways of getting to Newcastle in time for *The Roxy*.

Curiosity Killed The Cat broke their European tour to join *The Roxy* for a day to record their single 'Misfit'. Like presenters David Jensen and Kevin Sharkey, and new band Broken English, they had planned to fly from Heathrow. 'When we arrived at Heathrow and found there was no flight we had to do a quick runner by taxi to catch the 125 at King's Cross,' said Ben of Curiosity. 'The funny thing is that a number of fans had sussed out how we would do the journey and were at Newcastle Central station to meet us.'

Broken English had an even tougher problem, as they were booked to appear live on the first show. They were scattered around London in the morning anticipating a gentle ride to Heathrow and a lunchtime flight to the north. But news of the strike sent manager Colin Johnson off in a race against time, collecting the band from their various homes and shooting off up the A1 motorway in a three-car convoy.

'It was lucky there were no police cars

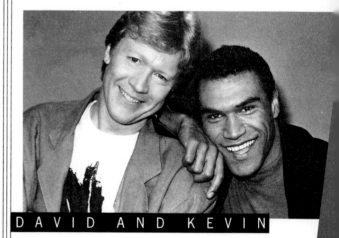

DAVID AND KEVIN

about,' he said 'as we had to cover 300 miles in four hours and then had only a brief rehearsal before playing "Comin' on Strong" for the live audience.'

Erasure, the first band ever to appear on *The Roxy*, anticipated trouble and travelled up a day early to rehearse their song 'Victim of Love', and Alison Moyet decided to do the same to record 'Ordinary Girl' for showing on the first transmission.

ALISON MOYET

10

But the people with the most responsibility and the most travel problems were the two presenters, Kevin Sharkey and David Jensen, whose job it was to link up all the bits with chat and keep the show together. David, whose radio show goes out on Capital Radio from nine until eleven each morning, planned to fly up at lunchtime for the opening press conference.

'It was the train or nothing at all,' he said. 'From Euston Tower it is a 200-yard dash to King's Cross and I just made the 11.30 train, which brought me to Newcastle only a couple of hours later than planned, and then the fun really started. The press were waiting and all the links had to be done as well as the interviews and the

Stock audience scenes had been filmed the previous night. In the twenty-four hours before transmission, director Gavin Taylor's main task was to marry these shots to the video clips and the recorded performances of Erasure, Alison Moyet, and Broken English, using presenters' links. He had already spent the night in the studio editing the Moyet material and the crowd scenes, pausing briefly for a twenty-minute sleep on the camp bed he had brought in with him.

With launch time approaching an invited audience, drawn largely from clubs in the Newcastle area, were dancing in the *Roxy* Theatre below the control box. When 6.30 p.m. arrived the edited programme

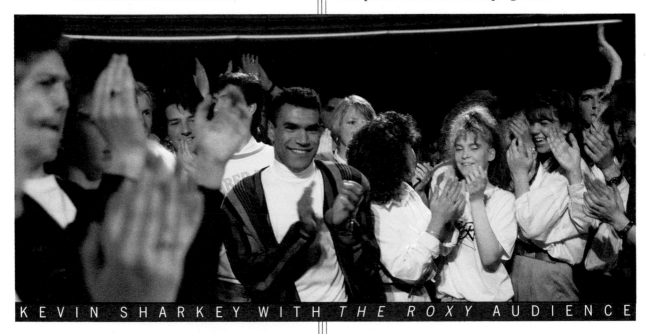

KEVIN SHARKEY WITH *THE ROXY* AUDIENCE

photographs. It was a wonder we managed to get the show away.'

Kevin had an even more testing time, finding himself stranded in Dublin with no flights and no money on the Sunday before the show. 'I had to get the night ferry then a train. The banks were closed so I couldn't get any money and had to go knocking on friends' doors to borrow the fare, while Tyne Tees fixed up a hotel in London and a rail ticket,' explained Kevin. 'Eventually I reached Newcastle at the same time as David.'

tape was still being wound on to its spool while a very resourceful announcer on Thames TV down in London, the first to transmit *The Roxy*, was calmly filling in for the delayed show by reading extracts from the *TV Times*.

'It was living on a knife edge and the adrenalin was just bursting out of my head,' said producer Alastair Pirrie. 'Someone shouted "For Christ's sake, play the bloody tape or we will hang." ' Thirty seconds late, the titles flashed on the screen and *The Roxy* was born.

2

HOW THE ROXY GETS TO ROCK EACH WEEK

*T*HE *Roxy* is a live entertainment with an audience drawn from all parts of Britain. It takes place each Monday and Tuesday at Tyne Tees Television Studios in Newcastle, and anyone with a ticket can attend and take part. The show normally goes on for two and a half hours. The programme you see in all regions on the Independent Television Network are recorded extracts from this show.

The bands and solo artists featured in the programme are drawn from the top seventy-five places in the Network Chart, compiled by the Media Research and Information Bureau – the same chart which is used with such success by Independent Radio on Sunday evenings.

The M.R.I.B. compile the weekly chart from recorded sales in 400 selected record shops around Great Britain. This system is as fair and as impartial as possible, and the compilers take great care to avoid any attempts to 'rig' the Chart by unscrupulous promoters. Another unique feature of the Network Chart is that it unites both Independent Radio and Television with a single authoritative chart.

The M.R.I.B. issues a mid-week forecast, which the *Roxy* team use to plan the Network Show for the following week.

Nearly all the *Roxy* staff are music nuts; those who are not have to grin and bear it or stick fingers in their ears, as new records are being played constantly in the office. Alastair Pirrie, the producer, will ask the secretaries and the cleaners, or even casual visitors, for a comment on a new record. 'Often one person will say the record is fantastic, another will say it is crap,' he said.

Tastes in music also vary among the *Roxy* staff, but all kinds of records are considered as the object is to cater for all popular tastes. Many of the records are pre-release copies not yet available in the shops, so that associate producers Sarah Lawrence and Ken Scorfield will already be familiar with the new chart entries.

'When we get the mid-week chart Ken and I start booking bands for the next

DEF LEPPARD

week's show,' explained Sarah. 'We can only do it provisionally at this stage, but we usually settle on four bands and then ask the record companies if the bands are available. If the band is from America, as is often the case, we have to give early warning so air tickets and visas can be organized.'

When the Network Chart is released on a Friday the original booking is confirmed if the bands have climbed the charts as anticipated. Sometimes sales of certain singles fall off during the week and the bands have to be told, as gently as possible, that they are out of luck. Sometimes there is a brief panic if both bands originally booked have failed to make the cut.

Sarah and Ken make their choice of bands and discuss it with Alastair, who makes the final decision on the four acts to be invited to *The Roxy*. Two of these will record on the following Monday with a live audience, and will go out on the Tuesday transmission. The other two acts will then record the following day in anticipation of their expected progress up the charts.

The bands travel to Newcastle to record for the show. Some choose to make the journey by British Rail 125, especially those who hate flying like Siouxsie and her Banshees. The majority choose to fly in from Heathrow, although Boy George prefers to travel up the A1 in his white Rolls Royce. The Christians were the first band to fly to *The Roxy* by helicopter. They landed in the grounds of the Gosforth Park Hotel after flying in from a TV recording at Alton Towers.

In Newcastle the bands stay at the Gosforth Park, a luxury hotel by the racecourse, the Station Hotel or the County. All three hotels have a reputation for being tolerant of rock and pop bands with their high jinks and eccentric habits. Not every night porter likes to be asked for bacon and eggs or bottles of beer or champagne at four in the morning.

David Jensen, the presenter of *The Roxy*, and his partner Kevin Sharkey travel to Newcastle to do their links and news items on Mondays. Their activities are organized by a stunning-looking researcher called Nina Donaldson. 'When they get here I have a meeting with them and give them the links they are expected to do,' she explained. 'They then walk around the studio with the director to sort out the spots they expect to work in. We discuss the final wording of the links, sort out the script, and feed them some gossip to run in with their chat.'

The selected bands normally arrive at Tyne Tees Studios mid-afternoon on recording day. Very often they are met by groups of fans, many with autograph books, who have waited long hours for them. Although many bands travel with their own 'minders', this is where John McPherson, head of security, and his staff take over.

'Most artists are pleased to sign autographs, and often the unlucky fans hand their books to my lads who get the stars to sign them later,' explained John. 'We have even passed over notes from girls to artists asking for a date, especially when Curiosity Killed The Cat are in. Nearly all the stars choose to come in by the front door. I think they really like the attention. Cliff Richards is different. He likes to go in by the back door as he will not meet his fans till he has his make-up and smart clothes on. Boy George is the same. He doesn't like fans messing with his make-up till after the show.

〰

'We once had a security problem with Paul McCartney and had to collect him from the airport tarmac by guarded limousine because of an Irish bomb threat. He did his show and we took him out the back entrance to his car without incident, but going down a country lane on the detour back to the airport the Daimler caught fire and we had to spill out rather quickly. Paul and Linda had to stand by the roadside while I arranged a relief car.'

Everyone who appears on the show is given the option of playing live, providing they give two days' notice so the extra equipment can be brought in. Few take up the offer, and generally artists either mime or sing to backing tapes. Bands do not normally bring their stage gear such as mikes and amps with them but use the variety of equipment that is stored at *The Roxy*. Guitar and bass players normally travel to Newcastle with their instruments,

BOY GEORGE

13

but drummers usually utilize the kits provided by the production staff.

By the time the bands arrive at the studio, the stage gear is set up and they rehearse the song they are going to play. This allows the directors, Gavin Taylor and Michael Metcalf, to work out the required lighting, sort out camera angles and arrange special effects. Once rehearsals are completed bands usually head for the canteen or one of the two pubs strategically placed on either side of Tyne Tees Studios.

At seven o'clock the audience are carefully ushered into *The Roxy* by security

CLIFF RICHARD

staff on the lookout for drugs, bottles of drink or cameras, all of which are prohibited. Then John Harker, the warm-up man, gets to work on the audience. You may catch a momentary glimpse of him on the screen, although he tries to keep out of shot. He is the best-known and most successful DJ in the North East, working a different disco club every night. John used to be a road manager with the Rolling Stones, Traffic, Spencer Davis, and The Tremelos, but has a liking for soul music and raves about Terence Trent d'Arby.

'On *The Roxy* I get the audience to point and clap in the right direction, and keep their spirits up when they begin to tire,' he said. 'Dancing is an important part of the show, and between the filmed sequences I play all the chart hits and introduce the artists when they come on stage.'

The 'live' bands play their hit number three times. The first time the four cameras in the studio are often working on long shots, then on the next take they get closer and work with individual artists. On the final run-through the hand-held-camera men move in to do those wide-angle up-the-nostril shots and the close-ups of fingers working the guitar strings.

David Jensen and Kevin Sharkey do joint and individual link spots, and late in the programme David does his memorized chart run down. Occasionally David or Kevin will go into the audience and introduce the band behind them, with John up in his disco box directing the applause of the fans. Once the first act has finished the stage crew build up the new set, ready for the second band. They perform their single in a sequence similar to the first.

The director controls the whole show from a box tucked away at the back of the set, talking to the floor crew through a radio link to their headphones. He does very little editing during the show and it is not until the next day, when all the bands have gone, that the show begins to take shape in the room affectionately called the Magic Cave. This room houses the most up-to-date equipment for picture mixing and computer graphics. Here all the best shots from the various cameras are wedded together with the presenters' links and synchronized music tracks are added to the film tapes. Stills taken from music videos are fitted into the chart run-down and the whole product is wound onto a reel ready for transmission.

The Tuesday night live recording is identical in form to Monday's recording except that the material is held over until the featured single reaches a high enough position in the chart to justify a showing. The edited programme that you see on ITV on Tuesday nights is timed to last twenty-four and a half minutes, allowing time for commercials.

3

THE PRESENTERS
DAVID 'KID' JENSEN

*H*E has an auntie who lives by the St Mirren football ground in Paisley, Canadian parents, an Icelandic wife and ancestral ties with Denmark, which probably accounts for his Viking instinct to travel and conquer. In fact, David 'Kid' Jensen, Britain's best known TV music jock, is a bit of a mixture, which he compounds by admitting to having supported Notts County, Q.P.R. and now Crystal Palace.

'I was born in Vancouver; my mother was a registered nurse and my father was a bus and cab driver,' explained David. 'He was also a jazz musician and a late-night DJ and was able to play jazz acts who normally had restricted play. In this way he got to meet greats like Billie Holiday and Miles Davis, so I suppose you could say music and broadcasting were in my blood.'

David did well at high school and was all set to go to university when he decided to become a music DJ after some experience on a local FM programme introducing classical music. He had studied music at school and played the trumpet in the orchestra. He also played in a pop band. Against his mother's advice but with her support, he sent off his demo tapes to Radio

Luxembourg, then the only successful independent commercial radio station in Europe. He also sent them to BBC Radio One.

'My tapes had a couple of commercials, some news flashes, a bit of music and some weather reports. Radio Luxembourg offered me a job if I could be with them within four days, so I sold my bike and my trumpet so I could buy an air ticket and went to their studios in London for training. When I arrived in London in 1968 I didn't have time to be homesick or be my normal shy self who never went out. London was the centre of pop culture in the world, and I went out every night to see a new band or to a club. A short time before I had been a kid in Vancouver, and now I was in London having a great time but working with people older than me. They called me Kid, which made me angry at the time but I quite like the name now. The first interview I did in London was with Ringo Starr about the Abbey Road LP. I also met George Harrison and went to Apple, which in itself was quite an experience.'

The Kid then spent a lot of his time working in the Grand Duchy, often visiting London to stay with friends. Working in Luxembourg during one Christmas he met Gudrun, his wife-to-be. She was an air stewardess, located there for the holiday period because of her flight schedules. Six months later they were married.

David's late-night radio show with Radio Luxembourg was called Jensen's Dimension. He stayed with the station until 1975, when commercial radio was opening up in Britain, then took a job with Radio Trent in Nottingham. He also started to do TV work, and hosted the Granada late-afternoon pop show *45*. 'It was mainly a performing show with a little bit of chat,' he said. 'Marc Bolan and Gary Glitter were going strong, and the Bay City Rollers were in their heyday.' Finally David received the telephone call he had long waited for.

'Derek Chinnery, then head of Radio One, rang me up and asked me if I would take over the sizeable boots of Rosco, who wanted to go and see his father in

California. As nerve-wracking as the prospect was, there was the excitement of having at last made it to London. At the Beeb I was lucky to be allowed a fair amount of freedom in what I played, although there was a play-list committee.

'I have always felt that if you take a genuine interest in the music with your producer, the programme can be shaped around your personality. I was able to play unknown bands like Culture Club and Frankie Goes to Hollywood. Frankie had no record deal when they played a session on my show. Trevor Horn heard them and signed them up. I was the first person to play a Police session, and Howard Jones was first heard on radio on my show and then signed by WEA. I once did a gig with an unknown band in a Cardiff high school. They were called The Pretenders, and I later played their first session. I used to get literally thousands of cassettes and had to decide which ones to bring into the studio. Times have changed now, and I don't play much raw music, mainly because at Capital I have the morning slot which is not the right one for new bands.'

David stayed at Radio One, where the Kid Jensen Show was a major success, until 1980 when, out of the blue, he received an offer to host a big news and chat programme in Atlanta, Georgia, for an awful lot of money. 'The offer came to me as a complete surprise,' explained David. 'Apparently the head of CBS TV liked a schools programme that I had done with the BBC about the life of Martin Luther King, and so I went to live and work in Georgia with my family. I found the work very interesting and the sort that I would like to go back to later. We had all the trappings of a luxury life, pool and large house, but as a family we missed all our friends and the quality of life which you can only find in England.'

Back in Britain, David rejoined the BBC and became part of the new night radio show, 'Night Time Radio One'. 'John Peel and I used to split the evening programme. I did seven o'clock until ten o'clock, when he took over and went through until

midnight. John is my favourite DJ. Working with him was exciting, and as a broadcaster I respected him. We often used to do *Top of the Pops* together, which was always amusing. He was my closest friend at the BBC.'

⚡

In 1984 David left the BBC to take over Michael Aspel's morning slot at Capital Radio and to host the new Network Chart Show. So successful has the chart show been that, in 1985, he won Top DJ in the *Melody Maker* poll, and the following year the Radio Industries Award for the Best Radio Show. 'The success of the Network Chart Show surprised me,' said David. 'Just about every independent radio station takes it now, although there is one near me at

Crawley which does not but people can pick it up in that area on Capital.'

In spite of being the anchor man on *The Roxy*, David still broadcasts each morning on Capital Radio. This makes Mondays, the *Roxy* recording day, a very busy one for him. 'I am up at six and get to Euston Tower at seven thirty, when I start going through the programme with my producer Mike Childs. We are on the air from nine until eleven, when I catch a cab to Heathrow for the flight to Newcastle. We get to *The Roxy* about two'ish and have a production meeting. We discuss the links and do a lot of gossiping and drink some tea. We sort out the positions from which we are going to do our links and sometimes rehearse introductions with the bands. Kevin and I always watch the bands in rehearsal, often from the

17

balcony. We start working on the show at about seven thirty and work through until about ten. Then we go to the pub next door, The Egypt Cottage. We have a private room there, where the crew and very often the visiting artists have a drink. Finally it is off to the railway station to catch the night sleeper, back to King's Cross, and on to Capital to start working on the morning radio show.'

David and Gudrun live in a large, modern house in Richmond, where one of his prized possessions is a first edition of *Treasure Island*, written by one of David's distant ancestors Robert Louis Stevenson. The house is full of many mementoes of their travels abroad, including a lot of heavy colonial-type furniture they brought back from Atlanta, and a lot of plates and ornaments that remind Gudrun of her native Iceland. They used to live in a huge, roomy flat overlooking Hyde'Park until their two children, Anna Lisa, now nine, and Alexander, now six, came along.

David's father walked out on the family when he was in his teens, which has made him determined to have a wonderful home life and that is why he turns down many of the evening engagements he is offered. 'My own formative years were not very happy', he explained. 'So when I had kids I was determined to make the atmosphere at home as harmonious as possible. I work hard and I could do more, but I don't want to have to make an appointment to see my kids to make sure they know what I look like. There have been times when I have come home late and the children have been asleep. I get up early and they are still asleep when I leave for Capital, and by the time I come home they are asleep again. Weekends are precious and I spend as much time as I can with my family, although I have to do the Network Chart Show on Sundays.'

David's big relaxation is football, and he is now president of the Crystal Palace Supporters' Club and a close friend of their manager Steve Coppell. 'I took up playing football when I was at Radio Luxembourg,' he said. 'We had a pub team which we

called Black Bess, and we took it very seriously and trained hard. When I stopped playing I supported Notts County for a time when I was at Radio Trent, because I felt sorry for them with Forest next door, and later followed Queens Park Rangers. They kept changing their manager and then put down that awful pitch on which you can't really play football. All it's fit for is ping pong and although I was a shareholder and a friend of the players, I stopped following the game for five years.

'Then Crystal Palace asked me to make the announcements at a penalty kick competition before one of their home matches. I really fell in love with the set-up there, it was such a friendly club. There were a lot of wives and children at the match, so I realized it was the sort of place I could take my family to. When they asked me to be president of their Supporters' Club I was thrilled. The only problem is that I get very worked up at their matches and really want them to win. It's a real relief when they score. I don't play football any more but I swim when I can although the local pools are usually too full of school parties to be able to get a reasonable swim. I am thinking seriously about working out, although I am naturally slim and don't have a weight problem, probably because I am so active.

'The fortunate thing is that music is also a form of relaxation for me as well as my career. I love all kinds of music, from classical to rock as well as pop. I think there will be a change in music trends in the next year. There will always be the sex symbol in music who will sell anyway, like Madonna or Prince; I am a big fan of his. Many people are expecting the return of the progressive rock bands aiming for albums and compact discs rather than singles, bands like Yes and Pink Floyd. Then we have the New Age Phenomena, not often played on the air but out there. There will always be a place for singles, for one-off novelty songs, and for serious singers like Billy Bragg. People are always naturally competitive and proud so there is always going to be a need for a chart.'

KEVIN SHARKEY

JACK OF ALL TRADES

KEVIN Sharkey – chef, deep-sea fisherman, carpenter and presenter – cannot remember the names of all the schools he was thrown out of. 'I was never violent, just a handful,' he says. 'The note to my foster parents always used to say "disruptive in class, could try harder, just trouble", and off to another school I would go. Eventually I ran out of new schools to go to and, at fourteen, I took a job as a trainee chef in a local hotel. My foster parents were also fed up with me so I left home and moved into a caravan. I had never done any cooking in my life but it seemed a good idea at the time. I started off as the dishwasher. It was a really disorganized place and after a few weeks I became chief chef.'

Kevin stayed at the hotel for a year and then paid to go on a six-week cookery course. 'After the course I talked myself into a job at a very posh golf hotel. It lasted one day. I made five hundred scones, forgot to put in the baking powder, and came up with five hundred bullets instead. I thought I had better leave quietly and sneaked out the back door and down the exit slope. Worse indignity was still to come, as I looked up to see the entire kitchen staff lined up and ridiculing me through the windows.'

Things could only get better for Kevin, who became a salad chef at the American Connection in Dublin. It was the local equivalent of the London Hard Rock Café, and he advanced to burger burner and eventually supervisor. 'I liked it there but I started to get itchy feet after a year and felt it was time to try my luck in London. Stupidly, I bottled out and changed my mind when I found a really good job in a very classy restaurant. That lasted only a few weeks before I got the sack. The Head

19

KEVIN SHARKEY

20

Chef caught me defrosting a chicken under a hot tap. Apparently that is the best way known to the world of causing food poisoning.'

It was at that point that Kevin decided to follow Dick Whittington's example and head for London. 'I jumped the Tube from Heathrow and arrived in Leicester Square with just thirty pounds. I wondered what I ought to do next so I found a smart hotel called the Regent's Palace, neglected to check in, and spent my first two nights there sleeping in a bathroom, slipping out quietly each morning. I saw an advert for a cook at the Hard Rock Café and went along for an interview. The manager would not believe I was black and Irish, but he gave me a job because of my brass neck. That was the first time I had a reaction from people when I said I was Irish, but it was a sample of what was to come. It is even more hysterical now when I introduce my girlfriend Tanya, who is very Irish, comes from Sligo, and is black.

'I was born in Dublin but I never met my father, who I am told came from Nigeria. My mother knew when she became pregnant that she would never be able to keep me, and arranged for me to be adopted. She put up a notice, "Good home wanted for coloured baby", and I was adopted by the Sharkey family, who have six children of their own. They found me a bit of a handful when I was growing up, but they always dealt with me as if I was one of their own and I am still part of their family.

'At my various schools there was no discrimination really, I was more of an oddity in a completely white community. The other kids sometimes called me Sambo, but I would just be rude back and call kids with glasses "four eyes". It was only when I left Ireland that I began to feel a bit of a freak.'

Kevin stayed two years at the Hard Rock Café before returning to Ireland. 'I wanted something new to do and I wanted to see Tanya, so I became cook on a fishing boat. I didn't do much cooking for the first couple of weeks and spent most of the time being sick over the side of the boat. It was a hard life, as you were expected to fish as well as cook, but I loved it and if anything went wrong with my present career I would go back to fishing.'

Kevin soon had the wander bug and once again decided to try his luck in London, where Tanya had a job in a Waterloo pub. 'She had separate quarters and said I could sleep on the floor of her room,' he explained. 'That sounded very attractive till I got there. It was a terrible place with no carpets, concrete floors, and some really rough customers. I stuck it for three nights and then Tanya got fired, so we both set off job hunting. I became a carpenter and electrician with a friend's company, making sets for video films. It was very hard work and I was exhausted by the end of each day, but I stuck it for two years and then managed to move into the design side of video. It was about that time that I heard about some music programmes they were making on television in Ireland, and I went over and auditioned. I was lucky enough to get the job as presenter, probably because I talked more than anyone else. The programmes were very successful and there are more series being made, which I am presenting.'

Kevin was spotted on the Irish programme by a designer from Tyne Tees who was visiting Eire on holiday. She told the *Roxy* production team about this very cheeky presenter she had watched, and Kevin was invited for an interview.

'I was in London on a short visit at the time,' said Kevin. 'On arrival I found two messages, one from Channel Four and one from Tyne Tees, offering me work. I came up to Newcastle and did lots of chatting and then some tests. They didn't have much time to get *The Roxy* going, so they made their mind up about me very quickly and offered me the job. Now that the nervousness of the early shows has worn off I am really enjoying it, as I love music and talking to people. Terence Trent d'Arby is my favourite artist, but I love Stevie Wonder and Marvin Gaye. My favourite band are the Eurythmics – Annie Lennox is a bit special.'

4

BEHIND THE SCREEN

MICHAEL METCALF
IN THE CONTROL ROOM
DURING A LIVE SHOW

THE credits on *The Roxy*, like the show itself, move very fast and the names of the men and women who make the show each week flash by quickly. TV music buffs may have noticed some familiar names, like Alastair Pirrie, Gavin Taylor, Ken Scorfield and Peter Bingemann. Alastair used to present *Razzmatazz*. He is now the producer of *The Roxy*. Gavin makes those brilliant music videos. He had two, on U2 and Queen, in the world Top Ten at the same time during the summer. He was also involved in 129 *Tube* shows and now directs *The Roxy* alternately with Michael Metcalf. Ken was on the *Tube* credits as associate

producer, and now he selects the bands and sorts out the problems on *The Roxy*. Peter designed most of the sets used by *Razzmatazz* and did some work on the *Tube* before taking on this new show.

You could quote the American president if you are the producer of a big TV show and say 'The buck stops here', and you would be absolutely right. The producer is responsible for the planning, costing, hiring, and decides what actually gets on to the screen. So, although it sounds like a great job it is a tough and vulnerable one.

Alastair, the *Roxy* producer, came into entertainment while still at school, when he played a small part in a production of Dickens, starring Adam Faith, in the theatre at Billingham. Later he worked as an illusionist and hypnotist before switching to radio and television. He worked as a producer on BBC Radio One and Two before returning to Radio Tees to run the music department. Alastair spent a period as a news reporter on Tyne Tees Television's own current affairs programme, *Northern Life*, before joining *Razzmatazz*, first as a presenter, then as the editor and finally as the producer.

It was Alastair and Gavin who made the final presentation that won the *Roxy* contract for Tyne Tees Television. 'We have always been dreaming about doing a chart show here,' admitted Alastair. 'A sort of fast radio show with continuous pictures and music, music, music. It all became feasible two and a half years ago when Luke Crampton, of Media Research and Information Bureau, told me he could provide us with a chart on which to base our programme. I told him it was an ambition of mine to make a show that would rival *Top of the Pops*. Once we had the chart lined up we began to work towards our own show and doing some serious planning.

LOS LOBOS

'Our first plan was to make it a weekly outside broadcast from an old dance hall in Tynemouth, but then it became more feasible to do it in the studio once the *Tube* and *Razz* ended their run. We took a chance on building the set for the *Roxy* three weeks before we knew we had it, otherwise it would not have been ready. If we had failed to get the show we would have been £70,000 down and left with an unwanted set. The technical format was no problem as we used a technique similar to the *Razz*, where you make three passes slaving cameras to VTR machines, and have post production editing with a fast turnaround. The real secret of the show is good camera work and clever editing.'

It is no problem to get bands to appear on the show as their appearance is invariably followed by increased record sales. 'You are under enormous pressure from record companies and management companies to put their artists on the show,' Alastair said. 'Our ultimate aim is to be a dipstick as to what is happening in the music industry, and to encourage good new bands who need just a little bit of a nudge to break through.'

A lot of the troubleshooting is done by Ken Scorfield, who takes over when Alastair is away and who deals with the visiting bands. 'I sort out the engagement of artists and musicians,' Ken says, 'and we pay bands, big or small, the Musicians' Union or Equity rate. Even David Bowie would get that, and the second-class rail fare we give to each artist. We also give them a basic allowance for an overnight stop, which the record companies can supplement for luxury accommodation for superstar artists.

'Our contracts people are brilliant and we have agreed a new deal for our artists, called the Backing Tracks Agreement. We have a cooperative relationship with the Musicians' Union. When an artist records the original track his name is listed then, when the tape is used for a performance on *The Roxy*, whether he appears or not, he gets paid for his part on the original recording tape.

(Tyne Tees picture)

CHRIS REA

weighed a ton. The reduction in weight of cameras has been the most significant technical development, because now you can have a colour camera the size of a cassette recorder. You can get the feel of presence with a hand-held camera because it can go into places that no other camera can get to. Technically, the wider the angle of the lens, the greater the depth of field or focus, so providing there is plenty of light the cameraman can move in and out without too much focusing and can work with two hands. Those amazing inverted shots of Los Lobos were obtained by the cameraman inverting his camera.

'I moved from being a cameraman to being a floor manager and learned all about the technical side of production. Then I became a staff director doing anything that came up, from football matches to church services. It was quite by accident that I specialized in music. Mike Batt, the Wombles man, came up for an interview on *Northern Life* and I was given a set of slides about the record before he arrived. So I went home and wrote down all the words from the song, analyzed the slides, and did some filming in the studio with the heat from a bunsen burner to get a heat shimmer on to some pictures of the desert. Mike and the men from CBS were so impressed that they put me on the mailing list for free LPs, and I was hooked.

'From then on I seemed to specialize in music, doing a programme called *Alright Now*. We had live bands like the Police, Dire Straits and artists like Rory Gallagher playing, and it led to us getting the *Tube*. That was a great series to be on and I have two great memories,' Gavin continued.

'One was of Gary Glitter coming on stage with a whole Scottish pipe band, and a crazy American glam rock band called Twisted Sister, who put on the most fantastic show.

'I then got involved in outside broadcast, filming bands. U2 and the Police played live at Gateshead and we filmed the concert, and that led me into doing music videos later. Paul McGuinness, the manager of U2, liked what we did at Gateshead and we

'I also get closely involved in the sound dubbing suite where, after the tape has been edited, we smooth out the transitions between the applause, the links and the music. Our improved editing technique is very much down to the British editing machine Tyne Tees bought specially for this show. It's called a Questic, and is incredibly versatile,' says Ken.

A number of bands owe a lot to Gavin Taylor, who has mastered the art of camera angles in a way that makes musicians look more interesting or more exciting. Gavin did not begin his professional life in TV or films but working in a coal field. 'I was born in Newcastle,' he said 'and when I left Rutherford Grammar School I went to be a mining surveyor with the National Coal Board, although it had been my childhood ambition to be a cameraman. My chance came when Tyne Tees Television opened up and asked for applicants to be trained as cameramen. I failed at the first attempt but was put on a waiting list and was called in a year later.

'I was a cameraman for fourteen years, and I suppose you could say I was one of the pioneers of the hand-held cameras. I remember when the first colour camera came it was the size of this table and have worked with them again. Later I did Queen at Wembley, as well as Dire Straits there and in Jerusalem, and also Echo and the Bunnymen. There was Queen again at Wembley, and Eric Clapton at the NEC, and more recently Freddy Mercury in Ibiza.

'The secret of good videos is to have enough camera crews, good positions, and to plan ahead. I always go and see the concert first and tape record it, and maybe do a rough hand video. I then have pictures and sound, and I take it home and break down each number into stage presentation, position of artists, drum rolls, guitar breaks, and where the lead singer is going to be. Then, with all the camera crews in position, I can sit in the outside broadcast scan and control room and tell each cameraman what is happening and what to look for.

'I have been involved in *The Roxy* since the early days and I would like to see it develop even more. I hope we shall be putting in more cameo off-set shots of bands intercut with their performance while they are playing. We shall probably shoot small videos in the afternoon with special set dressing. Anything to make it different and more exciting.'

The look of *The Roxy* is very much down to designer Peter Bingemann, who created the old-fashioned dance-hall look of *The Roxy* set in the form of a club for live bands to play in.

'Alastair wrote a dance-hall concept for the design and I took it from there,' said Peter. 'I decided that we could only do it if we went for one stage, as we had to have it up and running from scratch in five or six weeks. There were lots of politics going on and the final date was always being changed; at one stage it was set for September, which would have been easy. But it changed back again to two or three weeks. We had to move fast, and I did all the drawings and the designs with my assistant. I wanted the set to be OTT, larger than life, and the problem was getting the three or four firms making it for us to complete their sections on time.

'And there was the gold paint saga,' he said. 'I wanted a good gold finish and a sample I chose from the selection the paint shop sent up turned out to be from a gold paint tube at £3 each. The paint company had made their batch of gold paint for the year so I had to persuade them to change their production cycle so we could have our gold paint in time. It cost us nearly three hundred pounds and took hours of phone calls.

'The framework of the set came from a building company who do construction site girders but have a nice sideline in TV set frames. It is much better than scaffolding, and will take more weight and is more flexible. The proscenium had to be made as a mould very quickly, so we sent it down to the James Bond Studio at Pinewood, where they have a huge machine that takes out the

FISH OF MARILLION BEING 'MADE-UP'

air bubbles. Then their machine broke down and the job was held up. It was a test to get all the bits in on time. It was exciting and exhausting, but now that it is working we can concentrate on increasing the set area and bringing our second stage into use. It breaks up into sections and has strips of coloured flashing lights that all connect up.'

Working in the design office was Dave Richardson. He designed the logo for *The Roxy*, which is on the cover of this book. 'The lucky thing is that I trained as an industrial designer at Newcastle Poly,' he said. 'So I was able to come up with this shape, which is based on *Metropolis* and other science-fiction stuff from the thirties.'

5

A CHAPTER OF FIRSTS

E R A S U R E

(Tyne Tees picture)

THERE is an old picture of Vince Clarke of Erasure with his first band, Depeche Mode, in their Grammar School outfits posing it up for the *Daily Star* outside Basildon Station. That day Vince did his first Fleet Street interview with Rick Sky of the *Daily Star*. 'All pop bands have to be good looking to be successful,' said Vince. The *Star* printed up his quotes in headlines, and Vince was so embarrassed that he stayed in his room for a week, reluctant to meet his friends or other members of the band.

Soon after, Vince left Depeche Mode to form Yazoo with Alison Moyet. When 'Alf' went jazzy Vince, always adaptable, moved on to form his present band Erasure, with rubber-suited Andy Bell.

Many of Vince's fans think he did his most interesting work when he was with 'Alf' and, ironically, it was touch and go as to which of them would be the first band to appear on the new chart show. Vince made it past the microphone first by eleven minutes to make a little bit of television history.

There was little doubt in the *Roxy* production office that either Maxi Priest or New Order would be the first band to insist on playing live. Both bands know no other way to perform, and it would be whichever of the two that brought a new single out first. Seven weeks into the chart show New Order released 'True Faith', produced by

Pet Shop starmaker Stephen Hague, on their own Factory label. As expected the call came to Alastair, 'We want to play live.' This meant that the band would have to produce a perfect mix on stage to go out on transmission and to the dancing audience in the studio.

Two people were particularly delighted to hear of this request – stage manager Paul ste Croix and back line ambience man Clive Taylor. Clive is someone you cannot miss at *The Roxy*, a six foot three inch Geordie with a massive beard who returned home to live after establishing a reputation 'on the road' with major rock bands. He had just spent several weeks in between shows organizing the sound systems for the Capital Music Festival and looking after visiting Russian rock band Autograph. He has the job at *The*

R ⚡ O ⚡ X ⚡ Y

(Tyne Tees picture)

BROKEN ENGLISH

26

FREDDIE McGREGOR

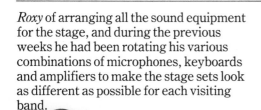

Roxy of arranging all the sound equipment for the stage, and during the previous weeks he had been rotating his various combinations of microphones, keyboards and amplifiers to make the stage sets look as different as possible for each visiting band.

For Paul and Clive the visit of New Order meant that the band would bring their own technical equipment to supplement the existing sound systems, and the stage would have an authentic concert look. Guitars and bass would be plugged in with cables, and the red and green lights on the black boxes would be flashing on and off. New Order are not the punk band they were when they played as Joy Division for three years. They now have keyboards, drum samplers and recorded backing vocals to supplement their live set.

Bass player Peter Hook, still a punk at heart, insists on playing his bass slung low below the waist like a gun fighter, and is uneasy about the technical revolution that has engulfed the punkers as well as the popsters. 'I am told that having samplers gives you more instruments and more variety,' he growled. 'I am not keen and I am sorry that we have had to write and record a song with Stephen Hague like "True Faith" to give us a hit. I don't like programmed stuff so I don't like this song. It doesn't sound like us. I like our own New Order songs, like "Perfect Kiss", much better. The only consolation is that we are playing "True Faith" live. We have never mimed on television and never will.

'I remember just before I joined Joy Division seeing David Bowie sing live on *Top of the Pops*. A lot of people called it a rough performance because of the sound but to me it was absolutely wonderful, with tension and real energy. We played live on the *Tube* twice and loved it. It is always tense, even for the technicians, because anything can go wrong and you get a real feedback from the audience. That's why I like *The Roxy*, especially when artists sing and don't mime; it's real music and it's live.'

By not having a record out at the right time Maxi Priest also missed out as the first reggae star to appear. Freddie McGregor had a massive hit with 'Don't Want to Be Lonely', which brought him to Newcastle from his Jamaican home to sing live to backing tapes. He closed his eyes and swayed as he sang his song on the island set in the middle of an audience that seemed to be swaying with him as one. 'I love this audience man, they really went for it,' he said. 'It takes me back to when I made my first live appearance as a seven-year-old in Jamaica. I was little Freddie McGregor then, and Bob Marley put me on a pile of beer crates so I could reach the microphone to sing with him and Peter Tosh. I spent all my time hanging around bands. I left school as soon as I could and had a hit right away in 1963 with "Why Did You Do It". The funny thing was I did not get a hit in England until 1982, and that was because of the Falklands War when I had just released "The Big Ship". It seemed that every time they showed ships at war or damaged ships with bits missing on television they played my song.'

When Broken English became the first new band to appear it gave an enormous amount of pleasure to Colin Johnson, their manager. For many years Colin had managed the legendary Status Quo, until a backstage revolution eighteen months ago forced him out. You can't keep a good man down, and Colin, with his partner Bob Young, very quickly found himself another very good band to manage.

Wearing their jungle greens and dark glasses, Broken English mimed their first single, 'Comin' on Strong', as if they had been playing on television all of their lives. The effect on their position in the Network Chart was electric. From being an outside new entry at 59 they shot up to 35 a week after the broadcast, and peaked at 16 two weeks later. Not bad for a new outfit with their first single, and due not a little to *The Roxy* breaking its first new band in its first week.

NEW ORDER

6

THE BIG HITTERS

GEORGE MICHAEL AND JERRY WEXLER AT MUSCLE SHOALS

SUPERSTARS like George Michael, the Pet Shop Boys, and A-ha, are like tail-end cricketers: they just love big hits. To them, anything less than a Number One spot for their latest single signifies failure.

From 'Wham Rap' to their last hit, 'Edge of Heaven', Wham dominated the pop charts of the Western world. Then

came the split, with Andrew Ridgeley going off to enjoy his millions and toy with Hollywood stardom and George, the more serious and more musically talented of the pair, setting out to establish himself as the best songwriter of his age.

In the middle of 1983 he slipped quietly into Rick Hall's Muscle Shoals studio on the Tennessee River. It was an unusual journey, conducted in some secrecy to avoid his army of fans in America. By jet to New York, then on to Memphis by another jet, then real excitement as he boarded an ancient six-seater piston aircraft. The low-level flight in the rickety stringbag over the plains of Tennessee took in a pass over Gracelands, the former home of Elvis Presley, before touching down on the grass strip at Muscle Shoals. There he was met by a six-foot-plus cowboy in high-heeled

MORTON HARKET OF A-HA

boots driving a large, bright red Cadillac, who took him along a shiny white road that wound through the woods to the studio.

Muscle Shoals itself is nothing more than a wide street with houses and bars on either side, but the studio has more prestige than any other recording studio in America. It was there that Aretha Franklin recorded her string of hits, where Bob Segar and the Silver Bullet band still do their best work, and where Rod Stewart began his solo career after splitting with the Faces.

George has always been a soul fanatic and was elated at his coup in persuading Jerry Wexler, the greatest living white soul producer in America, to help him record 'Careless Whisper'. Wexler was the man

leave when things started going wrong.

It seemed the age gap between Jerry and George was too wide, as George began to discover the depth and width of his own ability. He could write, record and produce with very little help in a very modern way. Wexler could not get the feel of the song that its composer wanted, and after seven days a frustrated George Michael flew home with a master tape containing Wexler's mix of 'Careless Whisper'. Back home George brought in Chris Porter to help him re-record the song. Released nine months later, it gave George a monster of a hit and established him as a major songwriter, producer and solo pop star.

George had discovered himself, but ever-sensitive to the feelings of other musicians, he firmly insisted that the Wexler mix should go out. It was quietly put on the market as a 12-inch by CBS.

Other hit songs followed but, regrettably, George's mid-summer hit this year, 'I want your Sex', was too overtly sexual for him to sing it on *The Roxy* where, meanwhile, those clean-cut Scandinavian boys A-ha were busy working on their Christmas special.

Morton Harket (known as Woodpecker), Pal Waaktaar (Po-peye) and Mags Furuholmen (Maggie), are not the first and will not be the last hit band to come out of London's Earls Court bedsit land. Pal and Mags spent a year there roughing it in one room, hoping and hoping for the record deal they expected but which never materialized. Disappointed, surprised and angry, they went back to Norway.

Fate decreed that they should bump into theological student Morton Harket, who had experienced second thoughts about going into the priesthood and really wanted to be a pop star. He was cleansing his soul in other ways by working with potential suicides in a mental hospital. He jumped at the chance of joining the other two and returned with them to Britain.

Morton was just the handsome hunky musical figurehead that Mags and Pal needed, and back to bedsit land the band went. This time there were three, not two,

31

who developed Atlantic Records and produced stars like Wilson Pickett, Clarence Carter, and Percy Sledge, as well as developing the career of Aretha. To George, with his vast knowledge of soul Wexler was approaching God status and it had always been one of his ambitions just to meet him. Working with him was a cherished dream that came true.

Every night after they finished recording George and Jerry sat up discussing music or eating in the local steak house. During breaks in recording they walked by the Tennessee River. Everything was set for a fantastic record, as George had even hired the legendary Muscle Shoals brass musicians. They were the first to

A - H A

to a room and a non-paying guest, a mouse from the basement as the resident pet. Then came their big stroke of luck. Terry Slater, one of the better music managers in Britain, heard their tapes and signed them up. A record deal followed very soon after and A-ha became the flavour of every month for a long time.

Because of Jennifer Rush their first single, 'Take on Me', failed by one place to get to number one in Britain but, like their albums, went gold just about everywhere in the Western world. Their songs are not inspired but they are perfect for the present pop market, as is their image as unmarried, pretty, trendy-looking, clean-living Scandinavians.

They are now very rich and have moved out of their bedsit into three superb houses. They still fly back to their mums and dads for Christmas dinner, and Morton indulges in his favourite pastime of climbing trees. They have a new album out early in 1988 and may play some of it on the *Roxy* special they are making. They are becoming more popular and hopefully, their songs will improve to be as good as their rivals, the Pet Shop Boys.

Neil Tennant and Chris Lowe write and record almost perfect pop songs, but behave and live more like the cool professional men they once were, Chris as an architect and Neil a journalist. Their detached, laid-back behaviour during their visit to Newcastle to perform 'It's a Sin' was no exception. There were to be no press interviews and no photographs. They wandered into Tyne Tees Television during the afternoon and sat down for a chat with old friends in the tea room. They were wearing the colourless, untrendy, drab clothes they were going to wear later on stage. Neil was seen to smile twice during the first hour, which is double his yearly average, while Chris fiddled around doing nothing much except to disagree occasionally with Neil's quietly voiced opinions.

'We like writing songs and recording but we don't like being pop stars,' Neil wearily explained yet again. 'I spent eight years of my life interviewing and writing about pop stars, which I think is enough for anyone. I really don't want to behave like one and I don't want to spend my leisure time socializing with them. It is bad enough being told to look like one, shaving and looking presentable and all that sort of thing. Being photographed and interviewed is also called for so, at the end of the day, I want to be as normal as possible.'

What makes them so agreeable as companions is their deep love of music and their obvious professionalism and attention to detail. They recorded their first hit, 'West End Girls', with the eccentric producer Bobby Orlando after Neil played him the demo tape over a Big Mac in New York. Bobby Orlando later issued it on his 'O' label, but somehow it never had much distribution and was only heard in remote Greek discos during the summer.

Neil and Chris, who still adore Mr Orlando, had to take him to court to get their record back. Through their new manager, Tom Watkins, they arranged to have it remixed and reissued by their new record company EMI. It is now history that 'West End Girls' became a huge hit all over the world and the forerunner of many more.

Success has made very little difference to their lives. 'I still am not rich,' Neil explains lamely. 'And I don't have a house of my own yet, just a flat. We only do what we think is right and not what other people tell us, so I can understand why some paper called us the rudest stars in pop music.'

When the pair left the Green Room to go on stage Chris still wore his peaked baseball hat and Neil his long shapeless green raincoat buttoned down to his ankles. There was no smile from either of them as their faces came on the screen throughout the transmission of 'It's a Sin'. Chris and Neil were just doing it their way, miming away in time to the music, hardly moving and looking as miserable and deadpan as ever. Somehow they must have worked out to perfection the right formula for writing and presenting their songs, for by the next week the Pet Shop Boys had yet another number one hit in the Network Chart.

7

THE VIDEO STARS

▲▶ T I N A T U R N E

TINA Turner, Michael Jackson and Madonna make the sort of videos that you can keep on your shelves, ready for the boring nights in the winter when you are marooned at home by bitter weather. They have the ability to mesmerize, not only by their performance on camera but also by the gossip and legends that surround their very names.

Tina has a particular affection for England, where she was encouraged to stage that very spectacular comeback after a period without success, fame or money. She chose to put on a series of live concerts in a small dancehall owned by Richard Branson, called The Venue, where she appeared with a four-piece band and two girl backing singers. Her opening-night performance was amazing as she strutted around The Venue's very small stage flashing her long, chocolate-coloured legs through a skirt that had minimal areas of cloth. She gave the sort of performance that superstars reserve for their farewell night in Vegas. The remainder of the week was a sell-out, with celebrities queueing up at the stage door to welcome her back.

Aided by Steve McCaughley, a sharp managing director at Capitol EMI, and an astute publicist, Debby Bennett, she was rarely out of the charts or the newspapers for the next three years. Hit followed hit. 'Let's Stay Together' was the first, 'What's Love Got To Do With It' the big one, and

her albums went platinum worldwide. The big question was who would be the guests on the Tina Turner 'Private Dancer' video, which was to be shot at the Birmingham NEC at the end of her tour in 1986.

Directed by David Mallet, the video was to use 37 different cameras. Eventually Tina, a life-long rocker, settled on old star David Bowie and rising star Bryan Adams as her guests. What is not generally known about that brilliant-looking video is that

34

although the show with Tina Turner, Bowie and Adams was shot live, the three artists insisted on staying on all night and miming to the recorded music from the concert. Toughened professionals, they still wanted to look their best on a video that was going to be seen all over the world. It was five o'clock in the morning before the three stars walked out into a grey Birmingham morning and back to their hotel for breakfast.

A few weeks later Tina was up at Newcastle putting on another show, this time for the *Tube*. It was directed by another very successful video director, Gavin Taylor, who had already made 'Under a Blood Red Sky' for U2, and who is now directing *The Roxy*. Since then Tina has made a *Mad Max* film in the Australian bush and bought a house in London. She will be up at *The Roxy* after Christmas with her new single.

While Tina's video was one of the most exciting, Michael Jackson's 'Thriller' was the most innovative, setting new standards in video making. By the time Michael was eleven he had recorded his first hit record with his brothers, the Jackson 5, 'I Want You Back'. At fourteen his first solo LP made him a millionaire and he topped the American chart with 'Ben'. He reached the number three spot in Britain with 'Rockin Robin'.

Then the incredible partnership with musician and producer Quincy Jones began. They made an album together called 'Off the Wall', which sold forty million copies. Later they wrote and recorded some of the music for Steven Spielberg's film *E. T.* on which Michael spoke some of the narrative.

The hits and the money piled up over the years, and it was not surprising that Michael came to make the most expensive video ever. It was for his hit 'Thriller' and backed up an album that sold more copies than any other album by a solo artist. Michael spent half a million pounds making the video, which showed him as a video nasty tormenting his co-star Ola Ray.

Michael drew greatly on his experience in making *E. T.* to write a fiercely frightening yet not violent video script, which was brilliantly directed for the TV screen by John Landis. John was the man who directed *Animal House* and *American Werewolf in London*. He relied heavily on Michael to create the fantastic dance sequences on the sidewalk that were such a feature of the video.

Michael has always been a good dancer. He talks of dancing half an hour each day, longer on Sundays, when he also does his weekly fast and cleans out his body. No roast beef and Yorkshire pudding after church for Michael, just fruit juice, nuts and a walk with the llama.

'Thriller' brought Michael into conflict with his fellow Jehovah's Witnesses because of the occult overtones in the video. However it did not prevent them turning up in droves in Los Angeles for the final concert of his last world tour. Michael had the last laugh on his bank manager too, if he has one; the 'Thriller' album sold fifty-five million copies.

Michael is now back on the road and in the middle of a world tour. He opened his programme on 12 September in Japan, and arrives in Britain in the spring. He has already had a number one Network Chart hit with his single, 'I Just Can't Stop Loving You', and his video has been on *The Roxy*.

While Michael and Tina set standards of creativity and sustained excitement in pop video making, there was a small, ambitious, American-Italian singer coming into the charts who would create a sleazy video style guaranteed to sell records by the million.

Just over three years ago Madonna Ciccone walked into Rex Studios in London's Clerkenwell Road, and asked the photographer if he would mind doing some pictures of her for the papers. She had a record coming out very shortly and it seemed nobody else wanted to know about her. He was smart enough to spot something in her manner and listened to the single she brought. He spent the day with her in the studio, doing both arty and 'poppy' posed pictures. They also spent some time walking around the streets of

Islington trying to take street credible shots.

A couple of weeks later Gavin Taylor and Malcolm Gerrie of the *Tube*, already renowned for spotting new talent, took a chance and shot Madonna singing live in a smokey Manchester nightclub. Two months later Madonna had her first near-miss hit single with 'Holiday'. An earlier single mixed by Rusty Egan, 'Everybody', had flopped. That was the last hint of failure, and the photographs from that photo session and the *Tube* film were to appear time and time again in subsequent years as the Madonna hits and scandals made the headlines.

'She was really sure she was going to be a star then,' recalls the photographer. 'She said I was lucky to have picked up on her as lots of people would be wanting the pictures very soon when she had all her big hits. She knew the sort of shots she wanted to do, although she was not quite as openly sexy as she is now. She was still doing dance classes, and did the splits easily and rolled around the floor. We went into a scruffy pub on the corner and she had some junky snacks. She didn't like England very much and thought London was too quiet after New York. She was in the middle of a tour of European discos to promote her single and she looked as though she needed some sleep, although in front of the cameras she really went for it.'

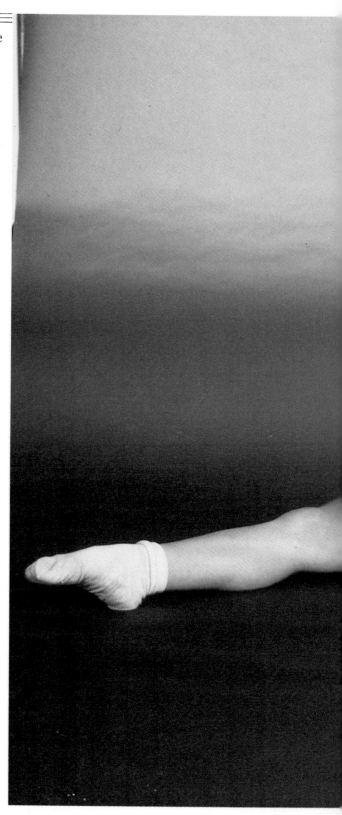

It was the same technique she was to use in making her very successful videos in the future. She used her dance training and her knowledge of the sexier side of life to make some very steamy videos. These got her talked about as a sexy screen star and worked up an interest in her records, which otherwise might never have sold so easily in such large quantities. In her case it would seem the artist is more important than the songs.

Madonna gained more musical credibility when she teamed up with Nile Rogers, the master of mixing rock with disco pop. Their first album, 'Like a Virgin', sold seven million copies in Britain alone, and was at number one in the American charts for five weeks. Apart from Nile's musical contribution, the video Madonna made for 'Like a Virgin' was controversial and tarty enough to make headlines in all the countries in which it mattered. It had a live lion and smaltzy scenery. It was full of sexy overtones and a few scares for the star.

'I was leaning against a post and this lion was supposed to walk right by me as I looked ahead,' she said. 'The next thing I know there's a nudge on my side. I looked down under my veil and he has his head in my crotch and is glaring up at me. I tried to out-glare him and he let go with a huge roar and pushed off. I was really scared.'

It must have been the first time she had admitted to being put down, for throughout her life she has gone for whatever she wants without caring much about anyone else. Two of her musician men friends, Steve Bray and Mark Kamins, were promised the production on her first album after helping her get a recording deal. Epic gave the task to Reggie Lucas, who had earlier spotted her dancing in a New York disco, her natural habitat. He made her first album, then lost out to Nile Rogers, who packed more artistic clout for Madonna when she got a sniff of the stardom she always expected. This summer, nearly four years after her visit as an unknown to that studio in Clerkenwell Road, Madonna was in Britain playing 'sell out' shows at Leeds and Wembley, and she has been hailed as the world's most successful female artist.

MADONNA

8
THE ROCKERS

PHIL COLLINS

THESE are the bands and artists who can easily fill the big rock arenas like Donnington, Milton Keynes, Knebworth and Wembley. They are also bands who generally carry too much stage gear to play live in *The Roxy* studio, but often appear on the show through the medium of video. Such bands include U2, Genesis, Def Leppard, Dire Straits, The Police, Bon Jovi, Queen, Status Quo, and artists like David Bowie.

Probably the band to make the biggest impact on *The Roxy* in recent months was Def Leppard, who chose to make their first comeback appearance on the show. So well did the Sheffield rockers perform their single, 'Animal', that it was difficult to believe that they were only miming. It was their first appearance on television as a band after taking three years to make their brilliant new album, 'Hysteria', with South African producer Mutt Lange in various studios in Dublin, Amsterdam, and London. One day Mutt became so technically involved in his production effort while he was editing a song with many different tracks on it, that he used two editing suites in London, miles apart.

Def Leppard are very much a live band, and they showed this on *The Roxy* when guitar player Steve Clark interlocked with bass player Phil Colleen and singer Joe Elliot worked up the audience. In the background Rick Allen, who drums with one hand after losing his left arm in a car

crash, looked as lively as he did on those huge concert tours that Def Leppard featured in across America four years ago. It was then Leppard sold seven million copies of their album 'Pyromania', bettered only at that time by Michael Jackson.

But Rick is not living in the past. He has a new, customized, partially programmed drum kit put together by Simmons and Zildjian. 'I started playing drums with Def Leppard when I was 15,' said Rick. 'Then came the accident, which left me numb for the first ten days. I started to work out how I could play using my feet, and practised on the rail at the end of my bed. When I came out of hospital I had a rough idea how it could be done, and I began receiving letters from fans and even some from one-armed drummers saying I could do it and must not give up.'

'We never even suggested that Rick would leave Def Leppard,' explained Joe Elliot. 'We knew he would come to us when he was organized and ready, and that is what happened.' 'The funny thing is that with my extra foot pedals and acoustic controls I can do things that a two-armed drummer could not handle,' said Rick.

40

RICK ALLEN, DRUMMER OF DEF LEPPARD

Def Leppard began their comeback tour in Britain as David Bowie was ending his world tour in Anaheim Stadium in Los Angeles. Backing him on that bill was former punk rocker Siouxsie and her band, the Banshees. They had arrived the day before from Tyne Tees TV in Newcastle, where they were playing their new single, 'The Edge of the World'.

Bowie has not had the greatest of tours this time round and ticket touts have frequently caught a cold. The music has not been as exciting and inventive as on previous tours or albums, in spite of having the gifted songwriter and singer Peter Frampton on lead guitar.

Bowie, now forty, has had a brilliant career that has embraced two fine films, *The Man Who Fell To Earth* and *Merry Christmas, Mr Lawrence*. He was brilliant in the stage production of *The Elephant Man* and, as a songwriter, has had seven number one albums in Britain and twelve in the top five. He has also shown great strength as a producer of other people's music. The last album he did for Iggy Pop, 'Blah, Blah, Blah', which had that superb single 'Wild Wild Woman', revived the career of the creator of punk to unexpected levels. It is also said that in Montreux, where the album was made, David taught the wild, wild, unconventional Iggy to ski.

While Bowie has been winding up his tour in America, another great British rock band, Genesis, with Phil Collins back with

41

the band after a lot of solo success, has arrived in the USA on their own world tour. They will not be close enough to Newcastle to visit for the next six months and have not had a good pop single since 'Mama', being more of an album band in the American style.

Their rivals Queen, prolific makers of hit singles like 'Radio Gaga' and 'I want to be Free', have not been touring this year. Freddie Mercury has been away with *The Roxy*'s own Gavin Taylor making an operatic video in Ibiza. Quite unexpectedly Brian May turned up at *The Roxy* with Anita Dobson, who sang a hit single he had

FREDDIE MERCURY

written for her called 'Talking of Love'. This was after meeting socially at a film première, when Anita arrived late and fell over his feet and on to his lap, and later into a recording deal. Perhaps Brian may get to play his guitar in the corner of the Queen Vic.

Among touring bands U2 have become one of the busiest, and possibly the best. In their homeland they have almost messianic status. At the concert they played in August in Cork, at the European end of their world

tour, they were watched by 50,000 fans at the Pairc Ui Chaioimh hurling stadium. Many fans had sneaked in by boat across the reservoir that borders the park.

Bono, Larry, Adam and The Edge played many of their old favourites like 'I Will Follow', and 'Out of Control' as well as songs like 'The Street with No Name' from 'The Joshua Tree'. Bono and The Edge brought their wives, Allison and Aisling, on to the stage to receive cheers louder than most rock bands are accorded in a lifetime. The backstage pass to have on this festive day was the one marked 'Family'. Here, every aunt, uncle, mother, father and cousin known to the band, with a few personal friends thrown in, were wined, dined and banqueted in a luxuriously appointed marquee.

When U2 opened the American leg of their tour a few weeks later, Bono and his pals could well have cast their memory back to their first-ever appearance in the States. It was in The Mudd Club in New York. The audience totaled forty people, thirty-eight of whom ignored the band and stayed at the bar to make arrangements for the rest of the evening. Those barhoppers probably wish now, as they too look back, that they had taken the chance to listen in such an intimate atmosphere to the band that is now the toast of America.

Headlining the Cork Festival the following day were Status Quo, who had spent the summer playing similar gigs throughout Europe. Formed twenty-six years ago by Alan Lancaster and Francis Rossi, when they were called The Scorpions, they were making hit singles like 'The Matchstick Men' when Bono was in diapers. Two years ago they retired from live touring after a career that had spawned

42

U 2

BON JOVI

thirty-eight hit singles and eighteen albums. Last year, after a period spent in litigation, they returned with a new line-up to support the Queen tour, and this summer they came up with a great hit single, 'You're in the Army Now'.

'The time away and the break-up has done us good' said Rick Parfitt, the former holiday-camp performer who joined the band when in his teens. 'There was no way we could have gone on, as the internal arguments were terrible and I felt by going onstage we were putting on a false front. Alan and Francis were in dispute over what we should play and what sort of image we should have, and I was sitting on the fence.

We wanted to play live again. There was an audience out there, 42,000 of them at the gig today, and we had something to offer. I never want to have the old band together again. Now we've got it sorted out, everyone has their role, and we have a lot of laughs. We have a new drummer called Geoff Richards and a bass player, John Edwards. All we need now is a couple of guitar players and we will be alright. We are going off to America next month to promote "In the Army", but we have a new album out at the same time. So if we get a hit from it, *The Roxy* will have to lash out and fly us home,' he said with a laugh.

Two years ago Bon Jovi were near the bottom of the bill at the annual Monsters of Rock concert, which is promoted by Maurice Jones and his partner Tim Parsons each August at Castle Donnington. They returned in 1987 to headline the show in front of sixty thousand headbangers from Britain's estimated two million heavy metal followers. During those two years Jon Bon Jovi and his New York band had several hits like 'You Give Love a Bad Name', and had shown it was possible for the metal boys to cross over and enter the pop charts. They have paved the way, and next year it is anticipated that rock bands will increasingly enter the charts and appear on *The Roxy*.

45

It was so bad that we were going to gigs in separate cars and staying at different hotels.

'The internal pressure had reached such a stage that it got to "Spud" [ex-drummer John Coghlan], and he left the band of his own accord,' Rick continued. 'Re-forming the band was not just a question of money.

STATUS QUO

9

THE GLAMOUR BOYS AND GIRLS

A LOT of the attraction of pop music for fans and followers is the glamour and fun that surrounds bands like Bananarama, Mel and Kim, and Curiosity Killed The Cat, or solo artists like Samantha Fox, Anita Dobson or Sinitta. Not only do they make good hit records, but they seem to make time to have fun and live a life of their own in spite of all the crowd and media attention. They can cope with the pressure and are still looking for further success, although it is easier to achieve now than in their early days.

Bananarama are a classic example of this way of life, as they churn out hit after hit like 'I Heard a Rumour', 'Venus' and 'Robert de Niro'. Managed by blonde Hillary Shaw, an East End girl who found she had a flair for both music and business, the band have become millionaires in a space of six years as artists. This has not deterred them from enjoying a lifestyle that always allows them time for a laugh and a drink or two and to be as unpredictable as ever.

Early this year Keren had a son by her boyfriend David Scott Evans, who stays at home to mind the baby and do the washing and the gardening – while Keren plays the pop star. Siobhan confounded her partners

46

BANANARAMA

by deciding to marry Dave Stewart of the Eurythmics before their baby was born. Their star-studded ceremony in a Normandy Château was the pop wedding of the year.

Meanwhile Sarah, who has no intention of getting married, having a baby, or settling down, appears at all the best parties in the best places having a really good time. She has a house-trained boyfriend David whom she says is a 'good housewife and a good cook'. Sarah is what is described as a 'one-off' – wild, beautiful, talented but a bit irresponsible. 'You only have one life and it is for living', she says. 'That doesn't mean that we don't work hard. We write our own songs, work hard on our videos and press coverage, and we do come up with hits although a lot of people have tried to write us off as dumb blondes. A bit difficult in Keren's case.'

Bananarama always work with good producers like Steve Jolly, write good pop songs and, since 'Really Saying Something' back in 1981, have had a steady stream of hits. They are acutely professional. They rehearsed for three weeks with Bruno, the Italian choreographer, for the dancing show they put on at *The Roxy* to promote 'I Heard a Rumour'. When they visited the Montreux Music Festival in the summer they partied most of the night, as is the local custom, but were up bright and early the next morning to shoot a fashion page in rolled-up jeans paddling in a rather cold Lake Geneva.

If you believe what you read in the papers you would have thought that Sinitta has spent most of her life going out with or not going out with David Essex, and would not have realized what a professional and organized lady she is.

Her mother, Miquel Brown, was a pop singer and the leading lady of the West End show, 'Bubbling Brown Sugar'. She sent Sinitta to the Legat Ballet School at fourteen. After Sinitta left she went into the chorus of three West End shows in succession: 'Little Shop of Horrors', 'The Whizz' and then 'Cats'.

Sinitta then landed a leading role playing opposite David Essex in 'Mutiny on the Bounty', where the on-and-off saga with David started, and where she bared her top half nightly as the native girl star of the show. Towards the end of the show's run she recorded a single, 'So Macho', which became a hit. The subsequent single, 'Feels Like the First Time' flopped.

'I was really disappointed that it had failed, so I rang up the Stock, Aitken, Waterman production team and asked them to write me a song,' explained Sinitta. 'Quite unbelievably they had read a story in the papers about me and my eighteen-year-old toy boy and they came up with this song, "Toy Boy", which gave me another hit.'

PEPSI AND SHIRLEY

Pepsi and Shirley came into the pop hit business with little difficulty after three years spent backing the Wham boys. They were the first all-girl group to appear on

The Roxy when they mimed to their hit 'Goodbye Stranger'. They had been well-used to travelling and working in a pop star environment as part of the Wham entourage. As a result they have handled their recent success and newly acquired star status without any difficulty.

MEL AND KIM

The rise of Mel and Kim has been more sudden and more spectacular. Pictures of them with their Peter Jones hats, stylish clothes, and model figures appear regularly in both the music and daily press.

Mel once used to model professionally – at least she bared her breasts at a lucrative hourly rate for newspaper photographers and became part of the Page Three cult. Kim has had a more secluded life bringing up her daughter, aged seven, but is now getting a taste for the glitter and the glamour. 'I am really enjoying singing and making records, especially since it is with Mel as we have always been very close,' she said. 'But I still love to get home at the end of the day to my family.'

When they make personal appearances to promote their songs, they invariably put on an immaculate song and dance sequence. They had this routine well rehearsed before they became successful singers. They even gave it a noisy airing outside the office of Supreme Records to

encourage the label to sign them up. Supreme must have been doubly grateful for the impromptu audition. It brightened up an otherwise boring morning in the office and spurred them on to sign the pair, whose first single 'Showing Out' was a big hit and went to number three in the Network Chart.

Mel and Kim are often seen around pop parties but are fiercely protected by their management, who make sure they work at their craft. To make the video for their later single, 'Respectable', the girls, already good dancers, worked on their dance routines in Pineapple Studios for two weeks. 'I could hardly walk at the end of the day, it was so hard,' said Kim. 'And I pulled a muscle.' They are yet another band to be parcelled and produced by the Stock, Aitken, Waterman combination, who seem to know better than anyone how to make a hit pop record.

Mel was not the first girl to turn her prowess at baring her bosom into a less obvious but more vocal asset. Samantha Fox, astutely managed by her father Pat, was way ahead of the field. Her big music break came when Clive Calder, of Jive Records, was washing his car and wondering who was going to make a good recording of 'Touch Me', which he was certain would be a big hit. He had already recorded the song, without success, with three other artists. Then all of a sudden the voice of Sam Fox came up on his car radio. He picked up the phone immediately to call her and a week later she recorded 'Touch Me', which became her first hit.

It was not her first recording. When she was sixteen she made what she called an 'awful single', with her own band SFX, who were for a time on the Lambourghini label. She left music to concentrate on her topless modelling career, which made her better known as a front person in newspapers rather than a singer with a band until Jive brought her back into music.

Surprisingly, Samantha has always been fond of heavy rock music and always fancied singing with a metal band. The legendary Lemmy, leader of Britain's top heavy metal band Motorhead, is one of her closest friends. She is not a wild party-goer but likes to have a pint with her mates. She also likes to dine out in style with her wealthy boyfriend, and recently went with him on a luxurious safari holiday. She doesn't throw her money about and is very well off from money made as a singer and a topless model.

The boys from Curiosity Killed The Cat have never been short of money either. The band come from well-heeled professional families and have never lacked for parties or glossy girlfriends. Now that they are Britain's hottest pop band since Duran Duran they seem to have more beautiful girls around them and more parties than ever.

Ben is very cool and discreet about his personal relationships, but together the band party in style with champagne and all the other trimmings of success, like smart hotels and beautiful girls. When they went to a nightclub for a private party during the San Remo Music festival this year, the police had to surround the club to keep away the thousands of girls who wanted to get in to see the band. When Curiosity came

CURIOSITY KILLED THE CAT

BEN VOLPEIERE · PIERROT

TERENCE TRENT D'ARBY

to *The Roxy* they travelled up by train at the last minute. As usual, the bush telegraph was working overtime and there were hordes of girls waiting at Newcastle Central Station for their arrival.

Their success has not been instant. They have been playing the club circuit for two years, during which the four members, Ben Volpeiere-Pierrot, Mig Drummond, Julian Brookhouse, and Nick Thorpe have become very close friends. 'Our problem is that the promotion of our music has taken over from the writing of the music itself,' complained Ben. 'Life seems to be nothing but signing autographs and giving interviews, which I find difficult to cope

with all the time. We are not a trendy, good-time band but serious musicians. You only have to listen to our first album, 'Keep Your Distance', or see us playing live to realize that.

'On *The Roxy* we really worked very hard on our four takes under the TV lights, and would have liked to have played live if there had been the time to get the sound equipment organized. We are a live band who play good songs to entertain. We are not a band to be seen as fashion leaders but as musicians. We do like parties but when we tour we try to keep the late-night parties down to a reasonable level. After all, making music, not parties, is our business.'

There are two artists who like to keep their partying and social life quiet. One is an established songwriter and singer, the other a rising performer. Both could be the megastars of 1987 on both sides of the Atlantic. Kim Wilde and Terence Trent D'Arby were both born musicians, but are different in nearly every other way.

Terence Trent D'Arby is yet another star thrown up by Britain's ethnic community, like Geno Washington, Lynx, Hot Chocolate and Light of the World. All made a minor impact in Britain but failed to make British Soul a viable international force. This ex-Florida choirboy, who has had an amazing impact on the music-loving community of his adopted country, could change this state of affairs. His first two singles 'Wishing Well' and 'If you Let Me Stay' were big hits, and his charisma and very obvious impact on women fans caused many sound judges to hail him as a British 'Prince'. He could well have modelled his behaviour on the Purple Pain, for he is reclusive, arrogant, ruthless and difficult.

Terence deserted from the U.S. army after becoming bored and was only saved from a long penal term at his court martial by an articulate defence psychiatrist who was able to declare him 'loopy'. Later he joined the German band Touch as lead singer. When they were about to get a recording deal with Ariola he signed a private solo management contract with K.P., Ariola's A&R man who is now his manager, and left Touch who failed to get their deal without him.

〜

Earlier he had quit a career as a journalist because, as he said 'I thought I was far more interesting than the people I was interviewing for my column.'

As a boy he was a Golden Gloves state boxing champion and very nearly turned professional. In spite of his lean look he is very fit and strong. Recently, when he was verbally abused and then assaulted by a large mouthy 'yob' in a public toilet, Terence flattened him with two blows. His album, 'The Hard Line', would appear to be well named. Terence also lived rough for a year in Camden Town before CBS signed him to their label.

Judging by his well-rehearsed recent appearances on *The Roxy* and at the Powerhouse in Birmingham, he is a very professional as well as a very exciting performer. He has not yet written enough songs to play a completely original set and draws on material by favourites like Sam Cooke, P.P. Arnold and Marvin Gaye.

He is disliked by many men, although he numbers Ben and Julian of Curiosity among his friends, and prefers the company of women. He reads a lot, is very bright, and takes time off to be alone. If he remembers that this is Britain and not America, home of hype, and modifies his arrogant performance offstage he could become the leader of modern British Soul as well as the housewife's choice for listening.

KIM WILDE CHATTING TO KEVIN SHARKEY

Kim Wilde was born into music. She is the daughter of 1960s rocker Marty Wilde, a contemporary of the Beatles who still happily plays gigs around the clubs, and was brought up very normally with her brother Rick in a country home near Knebworth.

After a year at art school (enrolled as

53

Kim Smith to hide her identity as the daughter of pop star Marty), she discovered that the pull of music was too much to resist and she went to work with legendary pop producer Mickey Most, who then had his own record label called RAK.

Her first single, 'Kids from America', was a big hit as was 'Chequered Love', released in 1981. Later on 'Water on Glass', 'Cambodia', and 'View from a Bridge' also did well but after 'Child Come Away' in 1982 the relationship between RAK and Kim seemed to founder and the hits ran out.

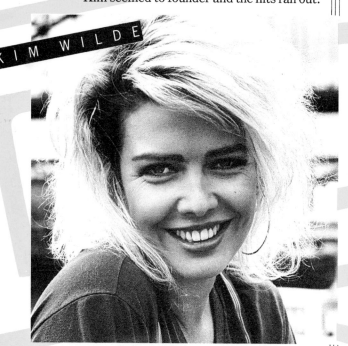

KIM WILDE

She did not fare much better at her new label, MCA, who had her styled and reshaped to conform to their idea of Kim Wilde. She appeared on her publicity material trussed up in shiny black leather.

Her album 'Teases and Dares' flopped. It was time for yet another rethink, and her mother Joyce became her personal manager. As glossy as she looks, Kim is a worker and a fighter, and she took a long time off to write more material, this time on her own as well as with other writers. In her new pictures she looks more natural, the sexy-looking girl next door. Last year she reached the number two spot in Britain with 'You Keep me Hanging On'. She later won the top spot in America with the same single, making her a dollar millionaire in the process.

She came very close again in Britain and America with her next release, 'Say you Really Want Me', which she sang on *The Roxy* wearing a bright red dress which plunged everywhere except off. 'Being raunchy like that is just a joke and to me a bit of tongue in cheek,' she said. 'People who know me well, and there are lots of them, know that I am very normal, but like a good laugh and that is what this is. Even the dress was not really thought out. I bought it for four pounds at a rummage sale and a friend and I share it to go to parties. At least people cannot complain about my middle-class look as they have done in the past.

⚡

'I have always liked coming up to Newcastle for the *Tube* and I was really keen to do *The Roxy* as soon as it started. It is always so relaxed here. I can go to pubs and clubs without being bothered as they are so used to artists. It is a real rest before going to America, where I will be interviewed for TV three or four times a day, posing for pictures, and flying from one town to another. It is quite worth it because having had a number one there means that I am well established and liked. All I need now is a number one hit in Britain. I just missed it by one place with 'Hanging On'. What I have enjoyed most in my career is touring with my own band like I did three years ago. I love live rock music and hope I can tour again very soon.'

Kim Wilde is the only British female solo performer since Sheena Easton (excluding Annie Lennox of the Eurythmics) capable of getting a major hit in America and Japan, where success means literally millions of sales of records. She is already a major star in Europe although the accolade of a British number one still eludes. As well as being one of the real beauties and charmers of the music scene in Britain, she has the looks, stamina and personality as well as the talent to develop and sustain her career as a major international star.

10

STREET CRED BANDS

ECHO AND THE BUNNYMEN

AWAY from the gloss, the glamour and occasional hype of the pop bands there are young musical outfits that try to retain their musical identity. They compromise only enough to get the odd hit, so some money will come in to pay the bills and give them a tolerable lifestyle. You can often still hear a hint of the jangling indi guitars in their arrangements, and their clothes are more akin to Inner City Road than trendy Covent Garden.

New Order were such a band. They had not had a hit since 'Blue Monday' until Stephen Hague was called in by their frustrated manager to give them a hit with 'True Faith'. They played the song live on *The Roxy*, with uncompromising leather-coated Peter Hook playing the bass around his ankles as usual. They have refused to move south from their native Macclesfield and are well organized with Factory, their own record label and recording studio.

Echo and the Bunnymen are another band who refuse to withdraw from their roots, and they run their now-lucrative musical business empire from a large rambling house on the edge of a park in Liverpool. It is full of boxes of rubbish and old instruments and equipment, and adorned with ferns and other potted plants which look as though they need a drink of water.

Interviews are not granted to visiting journalists or friends unless a few 'bevvys' are downed as a preliminary to a chat. The Bunnymen prefer their beer bottled in the old type of screw-topped bottles, which

THE CHRISTIANS

arrive by the case. Niceties over, the band will talk on most subjects but are less fiery than in the early days. Not so long ago, live on the *Tube*, Ian McCullough (Mac) their lead singer and main songwriter, interrupted a song he was singing to put in a short speech about cutting off a burglar's hand. He had just had his house burgled for the seventh time and was feeling very angry.

When the Bunnymen appeared at *The Roxy* to play their sparkling hit song 'Lips

The band had persevered in his absence by recalling their drum machine, Echo, and getting some help from drummer Blair Cunningham of the Pretenders. They all felt a bit lost without the unpredictable Pete and allowed him to slink back to the band with a minimum of fuss and disgrace. He

BLACK – COLIN VEARNCOMBE

appeared at *The Roxy* with a shorn head and a heavy tan, complaining about all the running and training he was having to do to prepare for the band's tour of America.

Fellow Liverpudlians, The Christians, owe a lot to the faith of the music backroom boys at Tyne Tees for their recent success. They had appeared twice on the *Tube* and were one of the early bands to appear on *The Roxy*.

On the day of their appearance to do their song 'Hooverville', about the American ex-President, they were recording a TV music special at Alton Towers, a hundred miles away. The only way they could get to Newcastle so late in the day was by helicopter and damn the expense. They landed in the grounds of the Gosforth Park Hotel before transferring by taxi to the studios.

Like Sugar', they were very happy and in a party mood. This was because their errant drummer Pete de Freitas, the only non-Liverpudlian in the band who comes from rather smart Goring on Thames, had rejoined them.

Pete had taken off on a lost weekend to the West Indies that lasted six months. As far as he could remember his activities while away included making an album for another band, starting a new religious sect and starring in a film. 'I can't remember what it was called,' he said. 'But I was one of the stars and it will soon be appearing.'

Not surprisingly, in their early days The Christians were mistaken for a gospel group. They derive their name from the three Christian brothers, Gary, Roger and Russell, who make up the band with songwriter Henry Priestman.

Another Liverpool artist, Black (Colin Vearncombe), made a first appearance in the summer. Black used to be a trio, then a two-piece with Dave Dickie. Now Colin has recorded a solo album, which Dickie produced, and Colin still calls himself Black.

All Colin wanted to talk about up at Newcastle was his visit to Los Angeles to sign his contract with A&M Records. 'I was sitting in the Managing Director's office when I heard this trumpet playing,' he said. 'I said "It is not him really, is it?" and he said "Yes, do you want to meet him?"' (The A in A&M, is for Herb Alpert, who co-founded and owns half of the company.) 'And sure enough it was Herb Alpert, and he showed me round the studios and played a few bars for me. He was dead chuffed that he had just had a hit in Britain and a number one in America. He was really terrific to me. He was extremely interested in what was happening in music in Britain.'

Getting away from the Mersey, a band from the Clyde also made a name for themselves. They were Wet, Wet, Wet, the hottest flavour of the month. They had come down to *The Roxy* to play their dancing number, 'Sweet Little Mystery'.

School friends Marti, Colin, Graham and Neil had been writing songs and working to get a record deal for two years. They were living on the dole and their wits in a depressed city. 'Wishing I Was Lucky', their first successful song, reflected the feelings of being unemployed. Only a few months later they were to get a real taste of success as they supported Lionel Richie on his British tour in front of audiences of 15,000.

Westworld – Elizabeth, Nick and Derwood – are a mix of British street cred and classy America. Nick was brought up in a Welsh village and later worked on building sites. Elizabeth, bred in smart Washington society, regularly rubs shoulders with the rich and famous at the American Embassy on national occasions but has hacked it round the more obscure clubs of Britain with Westworld. Derwood was brought up in the streets of Fulham and has roughed it as a labourer. He played in Generation X with Tony James and Billy Idol. Westworld have managed to have three hit records, 'Sonic Boom Boy', 'Ba-Na-Na-Bam-Boo', and the single they played on *The Roxy*, 'Where the Action Is'.

Then Jerico are another band of mixed origins; two were working boys and two were public school. At *The Roxy* they played their hit, 'The Motive', with a bit too much action. Few, if any, viewers realized that when Mark Shaw, the lead singer, threw down his guitar as part of the act he aimed it in the wrong direction and smashed it in half. He was heartbroken as it was a vintage 1961 Hoffner Semi Acoustic,

WET, WET, WET

THEN JERICO

THE KANE GANG

NEW ORDER

learned to survive,' said Mark. 'That is why I like having two members who went to public schools in the band, and why we dress in old smart clothes. It is the tattered "has been" look.'

Mark was twenty-one when he decided he had had enough of trying to survive. He set out to form his own band, Then Jerico. Already massive in Japan and wealthy as a result, he could afford to forget his origins but instead he still keeps his feet firmly on the ground.

The Kane Gang did not have far to travel to appear on *The Roxy*. They live in Newcastle and, like another local band Prefab Sprout, record on the local Kitchenware label. Their songs always have a lot of social relevance and their hit 'Motortown' was based on the experience of one of the Gang's sister who was working in the Nissan car factory in Sunderland. The night they appeared *The Roxy* floor was crowded with Kane Gang followers and tickets were at a premium. They had a big party with all their old friends in the pub next door after the show.

which he had had since a young boy. It was beyond repair and he is now searching the country for a replacement.

Mark is used to things going wrong. At 12 his father left him and his mother. As a result she was always out at work and he had to bring himself up. 'I went to rough comprehensives where they were short of everything and teachers got stabbed, so I

61

FOR THE TECHNICAL

ABOUT THE PHOTOGRAPHY

(Tyne Tees picture)

THE HOUSE MARTINS

THERE are three types of photography in this book: live on stage, candid pictures off-stage, and studio photography, all of which have their special techniques, characteristics, and problems.

Studio photography takes place in a tall, wide, special room fitted out with tungsten or electric lights. It very often involves hairdressers, make-up artists, and the use of cameras that use wide films to improve quality. The photographer can create flattering light to make the subject look very good or dramatic light to make the character really interesting, depending on the type of picture required. The studio shots in this book were taken on a motorized Hasselblad camera using a 150mm Sonar lens, which magnifies the subject and isolates it more from the background. The films have been either 220 FP4, which gives 24 shots per reel, or Fuji or Ektachrome 100 ASA film. A strip from the first roll in each session has been given a test development to see if the lighting is right for the film. In these controlled conditions you can also take a Polaroid picture through the lens of the camera you are using so you can make any last minute alterations before you shoot for real.

For candid pictures off-stage the big format cameras are too slow and too cumbersome for those quick, one-in-a-million snaps. For the shots in this book a Nikon FM camera, using a 28 or 50mm lens indoors or a longer one like a 105mm outdoors, has been used. The films used have been either Fuji 400 transparency stock or HP5, both rated at a speed of 400 ASA. Some photographers would prefer to use a slower colour film to obtain better quality but, for me, standardization of speed avoids confusion and prevents expensive mistakes with wrong exposure times. Flash is often used with these backstage shots, usually a Nikon or Vivitar speedlight or the reliable and accurate Metz CT 45. Out of doors a little fill-in flash helps because the style adopted has been to shoot against the light all the time.

The main requirement for good candid

photography in this environment are diplomacy and speed. To shoot first and ask permission afterwards might be a good idea, but it can blow up in your face. Shooting highly strung and very busy 'no time to spare' artists is a tricky and sometimes frustrating business. Most of them are very professional and regard press photography as par for the course.

⚡

Bands like Bananarama, Echo and the Bunnymen, and Status Quo, and solo artists like Kim Wilde give you a good laugh, while slick, organized bands like Curiosity Killed The Cat, A-ha and Queen just get on with it and finish it fast. Other bands like New Order and the Housemartins take it more seriously and you have to be wary. Superstars like Springsteen, George Benson, Lionel Richie and Madonna know they are stars and find it difficult to relax. That's when you earn your money by calming things down.

Shooting artists live in the controlled environment of a television studio is much easier than in outdoor concerts, where you are liable to get hit with a bottle or soaked by an uncorked bottle of urine thrown from the crowd. Exposure meters or through-the-lens metering is not much use here as the lighting is constantly changing. Very often you are shooting into blazing light with lights flashing on the subject behind you as well.

For all the action shots in this book except for those by Norman and Jack of the Tyne Tees TV staff, and Jonathan Storrs, who uses 120 format, a standardized technique with Nikons has been used. The 501 is perfect for fast action work. It has a wind-on motor, is very light, and has a bright viewfinder. Loaded with HP 5 uprated to 800 ASA, it has proved ideal. Normally the 135mm F2.8 lens has been fitted.

The colour has been shot through an F2.0 135mm lens on the Nikon F 3. This camera does everything except make the tea. It has through-the-lens metering, which has not been used, a forward-wind motor and a rewind motor. It is rather heavy but it does have a fast, accurate shutter and

excellent focusing. It is loaded with Fuji daylight film, uprated to 800 ASA. This means that the film has been given a couple of minutes more development to compensate for low light levels.

Sometimes you can shoot from the balcony that runs around *The Roxy*. But you are not popular if you shoot artists with bald patches from up there, although the Christians seem to like it. Flash cannot be used in *The Roxy* studio as this affects the workings of the television cameras, which are put out of action by the quick increases in illumination caused by flash.

Exposure time is arrived at by experimenting over the years. Generally the shutter setting has been 1/250 and the aperture F 2.8 or F 4. The skill is in pressing the shutter when the lighting is looking

63

THE SMITHS

right and the artist is doing something which catches the eye. At the same time you have to dodge the camera crews, who are trolling around on their wheels, and avoid getting on camera; the sight of a haggard-looking photographer in the middle of a disco dance does not make good television. It is very exciting but you have to concentrate and be very quick or you will miss the shot when it happens.

THE ROXY AUDIENCE

RESEARCHER Nina Donaldson had the task of selecting and inviting the early audiences to *The Roxy*. Before the show became a national success and the rush for tickets began, most of the guests were from Newcastle and the North East. 'I had the fun of going round all the clubs in the area and looking for the best dancers,' she explained. 'I found the most exciting and energetic dancers in a club called the Studio, where no one ever went home early. It seemed likely to me that if they were willing to pay to dance all night they would be only too happy to come along and dance on *The Roxy* for nothing. So I distributed most of the tickets for the early shows at the Studio. A lot of the original dancers still come but we now send tickets all over Britain. We also distribute to the art schools and colleges and other clubs in Newcastle.'

There was some national criticism of the early audiences for their lack of fashion flair, for which disco man John Harker had an explanation. 'The dancers from the Studio were all nice kids, but they were not flashy hairdressers, boutique workers or fashion students. They were working kids with not too much money to spend on clothes. Now that audiences are drawn from a much wider area the fashions and styles are more varied and exciting.'

Unfortunately there is a waiting period for tickets of two to three months but

THE ROXY AUDIENCE

anyone over sixteen can apply. You may ask for two or four tickets by post, because if you are travelling a long way it might be more fun to visit *The Roxy* in a group. It is worth making a big effort and dressing up in something exciting, especially if you want to be picked out and filmed by some sharp-eyed cameraman and 'go out' on *The Roxy* in style. But remember, when you get there you will be expected to dance your heart out during the entertainment, which normally lasts from seven until ten p.m.

WHERE TO WRITE TO:
THE ROXY (Tickets)
Tyne Tees Television Ltd
City Road
Newcastle-upon-Tyne
NE1 2AL